YOUR COMPLETE GEMINI 2022 PERSONAL HOROSCOPE

Monthly Astrological Prediction Forecasts of Zodiac
Astrology Sun Star Sign- Love, Romance, Money, Finances,
Career, Health, Spirituality

Iris Quinn

Contents

PERSONALITY PROFILE

Constellation: Gemini

Zodiac symbol: Twins

Date: May 20 – June 20

Zodiac element: Air

Zodiac quality: Mutable

Greatest Compatibility: Aquarius and Sagittarius

Sign ruler: Mercury

Day: Wednesday

Color: Yellow/Gold and Light Green

Birthstone: Pearl

The second zodiac sign, represented by "the twin symbol" and ruled by the planet Mercury. They are intelligent, communicable, and sociable. They usually have a good sense of humor, which makes them good communicators and conversationalists. Jack of all trades, they are. They easily adapt to situations around them. Moreso, they are very creative- they have ideas rushing in and out of their minds. They are the life of the party; excellent party rockers- this makes them famous. Because they are people pleasers, they go an extra length to please people around them, making them tired. They also find it hard to keep to promises as their attention is usually scattered. They easily become anxious and nervous; they love drama and gossip (Now, you remember that friend that loves gist). They have a dual nature, but one is dominated by the other; the other character is not visible to people, so people around them get surprised when they find out about their different nature.

Mercury

Mercury is known as 'the Messenger' and rules Gemini and the 3rd house. This is the house of communication and this everything Mercury symbolizes. Speech, written and verbal communication, music, and self-expression alongside reason, logic, intuition, rationality, the mind, intelligence and language- everything 'mental' aka to do with the mind and mental processes. Knowledge and the pursuit of wisdom are key traits for someone with a strong Mercury placement. You may deal a lot with emails, letters or communications if you have a positive Mercury influence in your chart. This messenger planet brings a practical and grounded energy whilst being mentally stimulating, wit-enhancing, cerebral and quick-thinking. Higher cognition, the imagination, original thinking, the simulation of new knowledge, concepts and ideas, and things related to authorship, journalism, speaking, radio, media, t.v or film, and creative work of all kinds come under Mercury's realm.

One is inspired to speak their truth, get honest real their feelings, and express oneself authentically. Positive associations include emotional intelligence, higher cognition, honest and transparent communication, intellect, and both intuitive and analytical thinking.

Month By Month Forecast

January 2022

Horoscope

Gemini will encounter problems and conflicts this January. You may struggle in life, and your problems are probably uncertain. What is important is how you will deal with it and make the right decision concerning just about everything.

In life, you will never know when is the right time for you. Whatever happens, make sure you are ready for the opportunities and prepared for worse scenarios. Try to be happy in either case because you will learn from them if you open your eyes and take the gist out of these circumstances.

In your life, you may expect to meet different people who will keep you motivated to be a better person.

Love and Romance

Try to be more understanding. This stage will put your relationship to the test, and your hectic schedule at work may negatively affect your intimate relationship.

Too much closeness with a co-worker is not healthy. You're giving a burden to your partner. Gemini, trust your partner because they are working for your future, and do not give them a reason to be jealous. Sometimes, our emotions are the number one culprit in hindering our success.

Work and Career

There's a lot of negativity in your working environment. Your company will struggle, and you will find it difficult not to talk and stand up for yourself and others. You will hate your work, and this may lead you to leave your company. Bear in mind that your company's success will be your success too. Try not to be the reason for the company's fall.

Instead, struggle as they face difficulties and stand with them through the trials. You may receive rewards for loyalty and diligence in the long run.

Remember that this scenario is common. You should know how to react to stressful situations. Learn how to manage difficulties lightly and with great encouragement. Be careful of people you trust when it comes to your finances.

Money and Finances

This month is the best time to save your money because all the luck is with you. Be wise if you were to spend more than you save. You can't just pick money elsewhere.

Invest in something that you can benefit from in the future. It will make you financially stable in the coming years.

Health and Spirituality

Gemini, you need time for yourself. Be realistic about getting things done for your medication. Even if you skip in some of your health routines, you must learn how to make it up and be consistent this time around.

Don't think much of your health concerns. Instead, pray and devote some time to meditation and self-love. Commit your plans to our dear God, and He will grant your desires if it is for your better.

Horoscope

You will feel sober and positive after getting rid of your bad habits, like drinking alcohol, smoking, and gambling. You will feel comfortable and alive, and you will see things in a better view.

However, Gemini, you can not escape your toxic relationship. There are some issues between you and your partner that makes you think twice. Although in your heart, you know that you are still deeply in love.

Love and Romance

Don't be obvious that you are desperate to find the right one for you. Take time to enjoy your singlehood, and improve yourself before the one meant for you comes along. You might stay single for the rest of your life if you continue being hopelessly romantic.

Gemini, this month shows you are so obsessed with love. You are chasing someone to love you. Please be reasonable enough and do not push yourself too much.

Although everyone might have someone to hug during Valentine's, it is not a day that only couples can enjoy. Be with your friends and have fun. Do not dwell too much on the concept of love.

Work and Career

Don't force yourself to stay in an environment that is destructive for you. Two-faced co-workers or over-competitive colleagues can affect your goals to succeed in life. You can become competitive for the better, or they may negatively influence you to fall behind and avoid conflicts at work.

You may leave when you feel it's not healthy for you. Don't forget, you know yourself, and you know your worth. Do not hesitate to quit if you know that is the best decision. Try to find a workplace that has a positive work environment. So, you can enjoy every bit of the day.

Money and Finances

With a sound understanding that vices will not help you succeed in life, you will focus on being in control and committing not to go back to your old ways. Make sure to avoid people who can lure you into these bad vices.

Your work is essential, and you will choose to work in the field that interests you. Thus, your decision may entail a degree of permanence of a pinch of stability. As you earn, learn how to save and spend only for those you need the most.

Health and Spirituality

Always make sure that you exercise every day. You are not getting any younger, so prioritize eating your meal regularly to get the nourishment your body wants.

We need to be content in life because wealth can not buy happiness. There are gifts you are blessed to have that you can not give away. Nevertheless, you can use these gifts to improve the lives of others.

Horoscope

This month of March, you may realize that you are more unselfish than usual. You have a big enough heart to share what you have with the needy. Your generosity has no bounds, and you can make decisions with the greater good in mind. There may be times when you are the recipient, but most of the time, you are the one who makes sacrifices for others, and you are willing to do it unconditionally.

Love and Romance

You must let go when it comes to love and relationships. This month's horoscope says that your love life should not be filled with what-ifs. Weigh your options and make sure you're with your spouse because you love them, not because of your background.

Giving up does not always imply losing someone. Consider this an opportunity to put things right. The correct person will enter your life only after the wrong one has left. Be truthful, and you will save yourself from additional heartbreak. When it's time to leave, do so.

Work and Career

This month wants you to stay at your employment if you don't have a good cause not to. You have a good-paying job, and things are going well for you at work; don't jeopardize your career with your laid-back attitude. We all get bored with routine things, but this is not the year to give up.

It is feasible to change careers, but you must be cautious. You must ensure that you have sufficient finances if you decide to change jobs or careers.

Money and Finances

You don't want to become involved in workplace disputes, and you're probably sick of blaming others for their faults. Slowly, you will be able to deal with problems in a more constructive manner, and you will be able to impact change rather than pointing fingers.

Proactive and effective. You will affect change at work, and your situation will inspire your coworkers. You will be in charge of your decisions, and you will carefully analyze all elements of life. Finally, you will conduct yourself with maturity and professionally.

Health and Spirituality

You may become frustrated while attending to your health worries, which can exacerbate your current predicament. Allow yourself some time to conduct the study and listen to the viewpoints of various specialists. Because your health is at stake, don't rely on a single finding.

There are treatments accessible to you, and if you keep an optimistic attitude, it may work well for you. Regardless of the difficulties, try to stay cheerful, appreciate your life every day, and fill your head with good thoughts. If your laughter and delight are genuine, they can help hasten your recovery.

April 2022

Horoscope

Gemini, don't expect much this month. Things will flow smoothly and quietly, yet it will all work out for the best.

You will live with a strong sense of self-discipline. Almost everything will be well-organized for you. There will be many parties and reunions for you to plan, so it's a good thing you're creative and talented. You'll be able to execute all of these tasks with flying colors.

When it comes to love, disagreements are inevitable. Singles may even resist entering into relationships, and serious commitments may appear frightening. To avoid this sensation, you must learn to trust and accept your blunders.

Love and Romance

April brings with it an unpleasant feeling that must be endured and cannot be avoided. It could also relate to betrayal and deceit between partners.

In the context of love, the month of April represents the end of a relationship. It can refer to a breakup, divorce, or separation based on trust, loyalty, and fidelity concerns. It could also suggest that you or your partner need to adjust an attitude or habit about honesty. If you ignore this issue, you will eventually lose each other, despite your love.

For singles, this could imply that you are still reeling from your past relationship. This tells you to let go of the past and focus on improving yourself.

Work and Career

Your horoscope cautions you about potential problems with backstabbing, gossiping behind your back, and badmouthing by coworkers and pals.

Perhaps your coworkers are attempting to bring you down. This could also signify tiredness or burnout. You may desire to leave your job due to a heavy workload or health concerns.

Don't take everything seriously, though. Everything happens for a reason.

Money and Finances

You are not doing that well financially. There's a small possibility that you will fail in business. Take precautions when taking risks. Avoid needless investment opportunities or do not invest if you have not thoroughly researched the advantages and downsides.

Health and Spirituality

Your horoscope would want to remind you to put your health first. The stress of your activities has had a significant impact on your health; you are physically exhausted and mentally upset.

The best thing you can do right now is to talk with your doctor and begin your wellness routine. If you take care of yourself early on, you will have a better chance of determining what causes your health problems.

Staying with your spiritual group may be difficult for you. You're definitely having issues with your spiritual leaders, but focus on your religion and be wary of others who pretend as guides you. They may appear to be sincerely interested in your life, but they are not.

Horoscope

Your priority is not only financial stability but also calm family life. Everything appears to be going well for you this month. All nice things will offer you good fortune and abundant blessings. Even if you do not pursue money, you will become wealthy and live a nice existence. As a result, money or financial issues will not give you a headache.

In an ironic twist, money might assist you in resolving conflicts with close relatives. A little assistance will make them appreciate you even more. They will adore you and protect your family as well. Your job will take up the majority of your time, but this is because you don't want to lose momentum at work. Even as a beginner, you are excellent.

Love and Romance

You will have a sense of security in your life, especially when it comes to love. Your connection will become more intimate, and your affection for each other will be stronger than before. You have a good chance of getting engaged, married or moving in together.

You will have a strong desire to be close to each other, and despite disagreements, you will find a way to strengthen your bond. You will be content with the love you receive from your lover in May, and you will be joyful.

For singles, you will meet someone who will flirt with you and try to make you fall in love with them. It's not that they aren't interested in you, but your allure has enchanted them to the point where they can't stand seeing you fall for someone else.

Work and Career

You will either advance or get promoted in your career. You will achieve your goals, and your efforts will yield wonderful benefits in 2022.

This month is a time of transition for you. As you bring more good energy into your life, you will notice a shift in your demeanor. Perhaps your haircut, clothing, or even the way you express yourself. You will choose to be someone who says and does things that lift others up.

They will appreciate your efforts to improve yourself, and you may even obtain incentives from the firm you work for, but if you are currently unemployed, these adjustments may help you find work.

Money and Finances

Geminis will achieve great success if they are persistent and diligent in their pursuits. You will see an increase in your financial situation. Being a professional will provide you with enough money to sustain your family, but it will not allow you to afford the things you desire.

This will be the difficulty you will confront in May: boosting your income through sources other than professional services. You will eventually be able to climb the success ladder and be able to afford a comfortable existence. You will succeed in your goals if you have patience and work hard.

Health and Spirituality

According to your horoscope, you should get an executive check-up to determine your present health status. If your health is bothering you, stay cheerful and constantly consider what is kind and helpful. Despite your health problems, you may experience a resurgence of strength.

You might be able to recover entirely in a few months. You will sense the warmth in your family in the setting of spirituality. You will enjoy the results of your forefathers' labor, and your family relationship will strengthen as a result. Certain family customs may be passed down through generations, allowing you to share your conservative upbringing with future generations.

Horoscope

This June, Gemini will experience a range of emotions. You can be quite skeptical about your lover while still feeling pleased and profoundly in love with each other. Relationships can provide you happiness, joy, and bliss. Similarly, when it comes to love, husbands and wives will experience genuine bliss and youthful innocence.

This month foretells that you will be showered with many blessings from God.
You will find solace in knowing that, despite a lack of material belongings, you have been gifted with genuine love and happiness.

Love and Romance

Long-term partnerships may interpret this as an invitation to take the next step and marry.

Capricorn's soulmate month is September. In the relationship, you will find harmony and understanding. Couples could even be given the gift of life. Those adorable little fingers will add purpose and fun to your life.

You could be expecting a child. This month could be the start of a new relationship for singles. The ideal person will appear and express his or her adoration openly. You might believe you've got a major catch but take it easy. Even if this person is everything you've ever wanted in a companion, keep your guard up and don't put too much faith in them.

Work and Career

You will be thankful for your job because it will require you to travel extensively.
Another advantage is that your family may accompany you on your journey. You will earn more money than you can afford to spend. As a

result, a staycation or international trip will not break the bank.

Working hard will bring you a lot of benefits. In a positive light, your company will value your input. You will be given an award as well as a monetary gift.

Money and Finances

Your optimism and sound judgment will help you excel in financial transactions. You will continue to invest in your fund, but you will be leery about dangerous investments.

In summary, you will not have any financial difficulties other than the ordinary expenses and obligations that must be met.

Health and Spirituality

The changes you've taken to improve your health are beginning to bear fruit. If you have switched from one type of treatment to another, make sure your doctor is aware of this.

Another good news is that your spiritual connection and positive attitude will aid in your recovery and experience miracles via religious worship and healing. Simply be honest with yourself and conduct a thorough examination of your health. Your treatment will be more effective if you get the correct diagnosis.

We frequently underestimate the power of our prayers. Ask for forgiveness with humility and acceptance. Your prayer has the power to perform miracles. So pray since you have nothing to lose.

July 2022

Horoscope

The month of July will cause you to move, progress, and transition, Gemini. You may decide to change occupations and abandon your plans. You will stand solid in your decision, even though it is clear that you are also pained by it.

In your life, something is going to change. You will be strong enough to make this shift, which will have an impact on not just your life but also the lives of those around you. You'll have to leave the comfort of your own house and go far. You'll make things happen, whether it's for your own personal development or a bold job move.

Many people will try to persuade you to stay, but you are destined to achieve your goals, and this month will help you get started.

Love and Romance

When do you know you've been abandoned? Is it necessary to end the relationship? How can love survive when you're separated by thousands of miles?

These are the kinds of questions that will nag you, and the answers aren't certain. You must make a decision. Your decision to leave is accompanied by a broken heart. A long-distance relationship is an option, but fighting your desire to be close to each other will be difficult. It frequently becomes more difficult over time.

As a result, this is a month of farewells. It's not ideal for long-term partnerships because it implies a breakup. Memories, years, and the future are all being let go of. Whether you are the one who is left behind or the one who is departing, do not stop loving.

In time, all things will fall as to how they should and if the two of you are meant to meet again, you will, someday.

Work and Career

You can find yourself on the verge of shifting positions at work. You wish to leave your former job for something more exciting because your current position appears to be boring to you.

Because opportunities will be accessible for you to carry out your strategy, you may be able to change careers this month. Maintain an optimistic attitude and prepare for your upcoming transfer. Consider the advantages and disadvantages before quitting your job.

In either case, you can develop yourself and it will benefit you, even if you decide to stay.

Money and Finances

Financial issues indicate that you have clung to a business or investment that you should abandon. It's fantastic to be comfortable with what you're doing, but if your comfort zone is already leading you to lose your possessions and property, you should reconsider.

Health and Spirituality

July indicates that the negativity in your environment is having a negative impact on your health, which could result in negative consequences. It's possible that you'll get sick or that your disease will worsen. If you're already sick, stay away from negativity so you can get better quickly.

Your quest for self-knowledge and soul-searching will lead to the rejection of your spiritual convictions. This month's horoscope suggests that you've gone through some difficult times in your life, but you're not letting them weigh you down.

You're busy with dealing with these life disappointments, and your desire for a quiet place to meditate prevents you from entering the spiritual realm. Everything will be lighter than you could ever think if you learn to trust God in everything.

August 2022

Horoscope

You'll attempt something new that is a little out of the ordinary for you. This month will be all about being a kid. You will attempt to playfully embark on your quest to self-discovery without regard for norms or limitations.

Gemini will have a carefree life while maintaining a cheerful outlook. You will demonstrate joy and true happiness through dancing, singing, writing, painting, and any other means available to you to freely express your feelings.

You have lost all sense of direction in your life. You have no idea where you're headed, but you trust that the universe will guide you there, no matter how crazy it turns out to be.

Love and Romance

When it comes to love, August will usher you into new beginnings. When you first begin your adventure, you will be more concerned with getting around and than concerned with your heart.

Perhaps the year 2022 will test your ability to be spontaneous. You'll want to set aside everything from the past and start over. Relationships with people you formerly loved will be part of it. It does not imply that you are locking your doors for the rest of your life; rather, you wish to preserve your freedom, and tranquility is your triumph.

You'll find someone better suited to you in the future, but for now, you'll be able to give your heart a rest.

Work and Career

You will come across employment opportunities that are completely unfamiliar to you. During this time, you may work while studying, and transferring to a location closer to your dreams is your best option.

You may have disputed at work, but the challenges you'll face will go away with time, and they won't have a significant impact on your work performance. Despite receiving a lot of constructive criticism, you will keep strong friendships at work.

Your organization will host a series of training seminars to assist you in developing new abilities. You may even have the opportunity to attend several training courses abroad that will aid in your career advancement.

Money and Finances

You're going to make a lot of money from places you never thought you'd put your money. Because your travels will primarily be for work, you will have the opportunity to earn money from frequent corporate travels that are fully covered by the firm.

Despite being overworked, your excursions will provide you with satisfaction. You were able to buy and sell things with these without incurring any expenses other than your capital.

Money will not be an issue for Gemini this month. But, when it comes to spending, be prudent. You could spend a lot of money on something that doesn't appeal to your target market.

Health and Spirituality

You'll most likely get an upset stomach now and again. You can get a stomach ache as a result of your openness to new experiences and desire to try new foods.

You're prone to depression, and food soothes you the majority of the time. Because your stomach has become accustomed to eating the meals accessible in your location, combined with your desire to sample new cuisine, it is quite possible that you may experience digestive issues.

Your journey to entrusting your life to the cosmos is an opportunity to disconnect from the outside world. Finally, you will be able to break free and choose to follow God's plan for your life.

September 2022

Horoscope

Gemini will experience a sudden twist in life, and it will be hard to figure out if it is for the better or worse. Set reasonable timelines for your goals. Learn how to deal with it, keep your aspirations at heart and your hand at work.

The twist in your life will affect not only your situation, it will also affect your family relations and career path. September has the effect of making you more eager and determined to reach your dreams. Learn to value humility, and modesty in all your dealings, this will definitely lead you to success.

Be mindful with your words, and be sensitive with your actions. Conflicts may arise among family members, and it can make things worse.

Love and Romance

September will be a pleasant start for Gemini. However, you will face a challenging month.

You need to focus more on what is practical and profitable in terms of business. Relationships with your partners will be smooth, however, there will be a time when the business will not earn enough. Conflicts and quarrels can be the reason for the closure, you may need to keep your cool at this period.

Couples may also struggle during this time, you will have to support each other through the trying times, but the burden appears to be too heavy to handle.

Do not let your mood swings be the reason for your break up. Because, it was too sudden that you were both caught unprepared. Try to talk things through, and let love foster between the two of you.

Work and Career

There's a lot of positivity and good working relationships when it comes to business. You can maintain it by avoiding negative emotions despite possible struggles in operation.
So, if you will ruin the relationship with negativity, chances are, you will not be able to execute business plans efficiently.
Remember that carrying out plans will require all of you to work together as a team.

The success of the business means financial freedom, so try to make things work to improve your status of living.
Appreciate everyone's effort since you will all need to perform significant roles to make the business prosper.

Money and Finances

This month will allow you to live comfortably. Your career is one of your priorities, and because you are successful in your profession.

You will be financially capable of buying a house or a car this month. However, watch out for purchases involving large sums of money. Ideally, you should save your earnings first and then purchase a property that you have carefully studied.

Investigate to make a good purchase, do not rely on commercial advertisements, post properties for sale in almost all media, trust your investigation. For instance, buying a car at a low-interest financing rate or a house in a strategic location matters.

Be alert, watch out for people who have evil motives. People around you will be aware of your financial status.

Health and Spirituality

Disease will recede for Geminis who have been suffering from serious health problems, there is a big chance that you will recover, and that is the good news for this month.

Take some time to be grateful to the people who were there to support you in your ordeal. Regular check-ups for the prevention of serious medical concerns. Now that you are doing well.

Continue with your healthy habits, and do not miss your medicines to avoid falling ill once again. Spend some time relaxing and enjoy this moment. Your optimism helped so much in your treatment, so stay positive and look at the bright side of things.

October 2022

Horoscope

This month indicates that you will overcome obstacles in your life and that the worst is about to end. Things will improve, and you'll be able to pull yourself together. You should be grateful to God this year for allowing you to avoid calamity, recover from illness, or, in the extreme, survive a near-death experience or astral projection. Because your prayer is so powerful, speak to Him more frequently.

Couples may betray each other this month, which could lead to treachery and deception. It conjures up images of backstabbing, gossiping behind your back, and badmouthing by coworkers and friends. This is a losing situation in life.

Love and Romance

You can be depressed or unable to accept the end of your relationship. This month may indicate that you have saved a relationship that was about to end. Be cautious, though, and stay away from dangerous circumstances.

It is not a choice to stay in an abusive relationship. You must flee the abuser and walk away from him. Consult a counsellor or seek expert assistance. You will lose each other despite your love if this situation is ignored.

Relationship links can be severed in some cases. It can result in a breakdown, divorce, or separation due to trust, loyalty, or fidelity concerns.

This may indicate that you are still reeling from your prior relationship if you are single. This is telling you to let go of the past and concentrate on becoming a better person. If you're single, you've figured out how to avoid being bitter at this point in your life. This could indicate that you'll bounce back quickly from a breakup.

Work and Career

In terms of a career, this entails severing ties with a previous employment that caused you to breakdown. You are relieved, and you believe it is preferable to leave your job than to stay and be constantly stressed.

You've come to the realization that staying in such a terrible environment isn't worth it. When it comes to your company, this demonstrates that you have revitalized it and made things work for its prosperity. This protects you from any financial hardship.

Money and Finances

This month comes with a cautionary note about workplace backstabbing or badmouthing. Perhaps your coworkers are attempting to bring you down. This could also be a sign of tiredness or burnout. You may desire to leave your job due to a heavy workload or health concerns.

You are not doing well financially. There is a possibility that you will fail in business. Take precautions when taking risks. Avoid superfluous investment transactions or don't invest unless you've carefully considered the benefits and drawbacks.

Health and Spirituality

You've been diagnosed with a life-threatening condition, but you're on the mend. This is wonderful news for your health because it attempts to demonstrate the value of life. You are making the decision to be healthy and happy today.

Make your health a priority. The stress you've been under as a result of your activities has had a significant impact on your health; you're physically exhausted and mentally agitated. The best thing you can do right now is contact your doctor and begin your wellness regimen. If you start taking care of yourself early on, you'll have a better chance of figuring out what's causing your health problems.

It may be difficult for you to stay with your spiritual organization.

November 2022

Horoscope

You'll have a wonderful start to November this month. Overall, you'll feel energized, lively, and alive. This is an excellent time for you to try something new in your work or in your romantic life.

Things may not go your way in the end. You won't have a lot of free time on your hands. You'll be working overtime and spending the majority of your time attempting to find an unthinkable gift for a loved one.

Love and Romance

This November, you will have intense perceptions of love, passion, and affection for your significant other. Your relationship issues will be resolved, and you will avoid future issues. It's also a good time to try to start a new relationship in this month.

It could also mean that you're stuck in a relationship that no longer makes you happy, but you're sticking with it since you've been together for a few years.

You have the power to alter the circumstance. Be assured that when you let go, the one who was meant for you will find you. As a result, it won't be as bad for you. Consider the happiness of the person you are releasing. Only then will they have a chance to be successful.

Work and Career

It's time to use your actions to take control of your career this month. Your innovative spirit, competitiveness, aspiration, and the desire to prove your worth to your employer via constant and successful work will all be boosted. Time management, discipline, and consistency are essential.

Make a well-organized plan for yourself and attempt to stick to it to avoid getting off track from your objectives.

Money and Finances

In terms of money and finances, this is the ideal time for you. There will be no unexpected cash outflows, therefore expect cash inflows from unexpected sources.

However, if you are excessively dominating, aggressive, or tough, you may have more conflicts with your coworkers, which will damage your overall success at work. You still have the desire to spend your money on luxury items because you will try to satisfy yourself in other ways. So, if you want to keep your financial situation in good shape, don't spend.

Health and Spirituality

This is the time to take large risks in order to break your bad habits. Make an effort to exercise and live a healthy lifestyle. Start a new habit by paying attention to what you consume on a regular basis. Be aware of your loved ones' health worries and symptoms, especially if they have had previous illnesses. Try to find alternative treatments for persistent ailments.

December 2022

Horoscope

Not everyone who works hard is rewarded. We'll also need a little luck to succeed. This month, Geminis will receive what they sow, but you may want to celebrate in secret.

The month of December will offer excellent news at work. You will be recognized by higher-ups, but your colleagues, motivated by their own aspirations, will try to dull your light.

Everyone enjoys a good romance, and you will have one this month. But be cautious since, under the influence of Aquarius, even if you two become close, the relationship may not continue. However, if they settle down and get to know each other better, a lifetime commitment is still conceivable.

Love and Romance

Geminis are known for their coldness in romantic relationships. Except for this month, it is correct. Regardless of the deceit, you will meet someone who will win your heart, and there will be no way for you to disguise your feelings.

Your personality looks to be demanding and authoritative, yet with your heightened emotions, you may want to start a relationship right soon. Take a deep breath, my dear. Don't make a hasty decision regarding something you'll have to live with for the rest of your life. Your aggression has the potential to lead you astray.

You will fall passionately in love, but don't get too worked up over it because chances are you won't end up together.

Work and Career

Progress in your career will be modest this year as well.

Your superiors will notice your efforts if you are patient and dedicated. However, do not brag about your accomplishments at work because your coworkers may get envious of you. To avoid unhealthy rivalry at work, celebrate your achievement with your family.

Your career development will not always be easy. If your workplace becomes unpleasant, quit. Backstabbers are like garbage: they're everywhere. So, get away from them, or you'll stink too. In any case, no one likes toxic coworkers.

Money and Finances

This month, fortune favors you. Your company will improve, and financial stability will be attained.

It is correct not to be greedy, but while spending on family celebrations, remember not to overspend. Develop excellent budgeting habits. Avoid spending triggers such as sale goods on your way to work, and turn off your shopping app alerts if it is not your regular shopping day for essentials.

Do not confuse new goods for a happy pill; instead, spend money on things that may boost your soul, things that you can splurge on, and your money will not have been squandered, such as important vacations and experiences.

Health and Spirituality

In terms of health, December is a good month for Gemini; you'll be in good physical, emotional, and mental shape this year.

Keep a record of your dietary habits. Examine what you eat on a regular basis and what you should be eating, and gradually transition from your old plate to a more balanced one. Otherwise, you may get digestive issues. Incorporate dairy and veggies into your diet. Reduced alcohol intake will also aid in the preservation of your health.

Regularly meditate to re-establish equilibrium in your life. December is associated with the prospect of being cut off from the rest of the cosmos. Your hectic lifestyle may be preventing you from discovering the spiritual path.

Printed in Great Britain
by Amazon